Dance

Swing Dance

By Trudy Becker

level 2
little blue readers

www.littlebluehousebooks.com

Little Blue House is distributed by North Star Editions:
sales@northstareditions.com | 888-417-0195

Produced for Little Blue House by Red Line Editorial.

Photographs ©: iStockphoto, cover, 4, 13, 19; Shutterstock Images, 7, 9, 10, 14–15, 16, 21, 23, 24 (top left), 24 (top right), 24 (bottom left), 24 (bottom right)

Library of Congress Control Number: 2022919987

ISBN
978-1-64619-832-0 (hardcover)
978-1-64619-861-0 (paperback)
978-1-64619-916-7 (ebook pdf)
978-1-64619-890-0 (hosted ebook)

Printed in the United States of America
Mankato, MN
082023

About the Author

Trudy Becker lives in Minneapolis, Minnesota. She likes exploring new places and loves anything involving books.

Table of Contents

Dancing Pairs

Two dancers join their hands. They spin around the floor. They add kicks and turns to their dance.

Another pair
moves quickly.
They are fast, and their
steps are light.
They are great at
working together.

pair

Two dancers do a lift.

They enjoy the fun music.

They are swing dancing.

lift

All About It

Swing dance started in
New York City.
Dancers move to
swing music.
That is a kind of jazz.

Many partner dances are types of swing dance. Partners hold hands and move fast to the beat. They do turns, flips, and jumps.

Swing dance is a social dance.
That means it happens for fun and in groups.
Swing dancers can do it in a crowd.

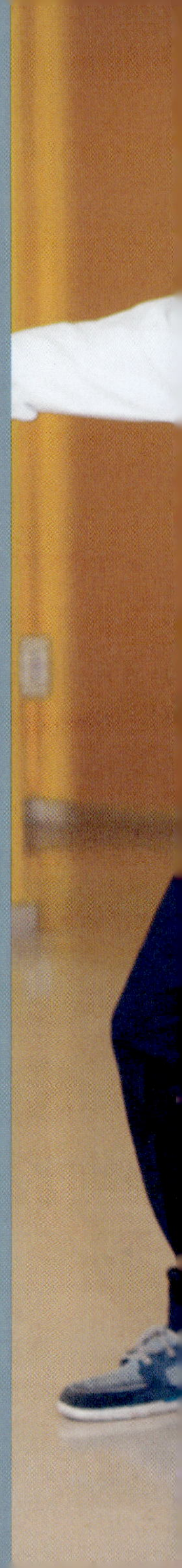

Learning How

Swing dancers practice. Sometimes they dance with partners they know. Other times, they dance with new people.

Dancers use the same basic moves, but they can dance in their own ways. That makes it more fun to perform or compete.

Swing dancers can wear flowing skirts or pants. They usually wear hard shoes. That makes it easier to step and turn.

skirt

Before dancing, dancers get ready.
They stretch their bodies and check with their partners.
It is time to swing dance!

Glossary

lift

skirt

pair

stretch

Index